MW01268189

PRAISE FOR
HOPE HAVEN

66 When Jane and I enrolled our daughter Linda in Hope Haven's school, we were immediately impressed with the ability and commitment of the teachers in helping her to learn and progress.

Today, over 40 years later, Linda has community based employment, lives independently, and is an active member of her church and community.

As a current board member, I have observed multiple changes in the size and scope of Hope Haven, but the commitment to excellence in serving individuals with disabilities continues."

— RON BOOTE—
HOPE HAVEN BOARD PRESIDENT

66 We have been privileged to participate in Hope Haven's international wheelchair ministry for several years. It's success is closely linked to the humility with which it serves the less fortunate. It equates to pure joy, both for the receiver as well as the giver."

— OMAR ALEMAN —
ALEMAN & ASSOCIATES, VP

" Hope Haven, Inc. has always been a progressive industry leader that cares about its clients, families, employees, and communities. I recall the year Rock Valley experienced historic flooding. It was the same year they were to have hosted RAGBRAI. Hope Haven had clients and families that were displaced for weeks as a result of this flooding.

The Hope Haven and Rock Valley community quickly found housing for all their clients, working closely with the local college, supported the community to assist neighbors and friends that were displaced, and were able to host the event! It was truly an experience that showed Hope Haven's full integration and participation in the community!"

— SHELLY CHANDLER —
CHIEF EXECUTIVE OFFICER,
IOWA ASSOCIATION OF COMMUNITY PROVIDERS

" Over the past 50+ years I have seen Hope Haven greatly impacting lives in so many ways. From the early years serving children with disabilities including my wonderful brother Harlan who was born with cerebral palsy....to later helping disabled adults find meaning and opportunity in work, and eventually to providing wheelchairs across the world to those in need.

All of this started with "What can we do to help?" An amazing history and legacy of serving God through caring for disabled children and adults locally and internationally."

— CARL WYNJA —
REGIONAL PRESIDENT,
COMMUNITY BANKING, US BANK

66 When Harvey De Jager asked me to serve as Hope Haven's treasurer in the early 1980's, I gladly said yes. I was a relatively new businessman in Rock Valley, pleased to get some exposure outside of my office, and pleased to find a volunteer position that utilized my skills.

Little did I know that the work of Hope Haven would have a profound effect on me. I became acquainted with many staff and clients. I began to know them as people. It amazed me how the staff and clients worked together to enrich each other's lives. I learned that Hope Haven really does help people "...reach their full potential and find dignity through work."

When the Hope Haven Support Foundation was formed in 1989, I was asked to serve as its President. In that capacity I have learned another aspect of Hope Haven's community - the generosity and support of their far reaching community of supporters.

Hope Haven has had a positive effect on this entire region, but especially on the staff, board members, clients, and supporters. Hope Haven is a testimony of God's faithfulness. I am proud to have been a volunteer for over half of the years of Hope Haven's existence."

— JOE VAN TOL —
CHAIRMAN, PEOPLES BANK

66 This book captures the stories of families and friends who share the burdens of care for those with mental and physical disabilities. As a brother to one of those subjects, I am unable to sufficiently express in words the value and emotional worth of what Hope Haven provided for him. He learned improved personal hygiene, discipline, responsibilities and obedience in identifying himself as a worthwhile human being, able to be of help in selected activities, and better able to communicate with others. Bricks and mortar help provide for this, but the actual reality for those attributes to functionally occur and develop in a person with restricted mental capacities is miraculous. My brother received that miracle. This book identifies how those actions can come about through the work and devotion of dedicated teachers and staff.

For those with limited mental and physical capabilities, it is a challenge to devise ways to increase the sense of worth, dignity and demeanor in personal day-to-day living for them. This book expertly captures the difficulties and rewards in how education in a safe work environment can bring out the true character of those with limited skills. After reading this book, one's understanding of human nature will not be the same."

— DONALD W NIBBELINK —
M.D., PH.D.

66 Hope Haven and I have had a fantastic relationship for over 40 years. It began while I was employed by Iowa Department Of Human Services. After retiring from DHS, I worked for Hope Haven because of it's passion and faith based commitment to serving people with disabilities."

— DENNIS SASSMAN —
M.S.W, FORMER RESIDENTIAL MANAGER

66 Since starting the Los Cabos Children's Foundation, Hope Haven has changed the world for over 375 children on the Baja Peninsula. Without mobility, children can't go to school. Hope Haven's story is inspirational to the impact caring, committed people can have throughout the world."

— THOMAS WALSH SR. —
CEO CHAIRMAN, GREATLIFE GOLF AND FITNESS

Hope Haven is based on a Christ-centered mission that believes every person in society is an image-bearer of God. Under Hope Haven's vision, each person is created for a purpose and a reason at a specific time in the world. Over the decades, the organization has helped thousands of clients aspire in carrying out God's kingdom plan by embracing each person's unique skills, traits, and abilities.

— RANDY FEENSTRA —
IOWA STATE SENATOR

Hope Haven has been a part of my vocabulary for 40 years. In that time, their growth and commitment to people with disabilities has been right on point to meet people where they are. Most importantly, they have remained true to their spiritual calling."

— SCOTT LAWRENCE
PRESIDENT, CEO, LAWRENCE & SCHILLER

“ I can trace my heartwarming relationship with Hope Haven back to the 1980s when I first visited its campus. I was impressed with the many ways it was reaching out and supporting people with disabilities – and doing it with joy and excellence. Little did I dream then that Joni and Friends would one day partner with this extraordinary organization. From the very beginning of our Wheels for the World outreach, Hope Haven was there, supporting our volunteers and helping to restore wheelchairs for our outreaches. Even now, decades later, our ministry utilizes Hope Haven's exceptional pediatric wheelchairs to meet the needs of children with disabilities across the globe. But Hope Haven is about more than just wheelchairs – it's about community living, spiritual support, employment opportunities, advocacy and more. I have long admired and respected the commitment of my good friends at Hope Haven as they strive to make a huge difference in the lives of people with disabilities in the name of Christ, whether here in the US or abroad. And now? I'm grateful to God that it's all cataloged in this wonderful new book – read it and be amazed at how God's hand has grown, guided, and blessed the work of this outstanding outreach!"

— JONI EARECKSON TADA—
JONI AND FRIENDS INTERNATIONAL DISABILITY CENTER

HOPE HAVEN

Hope in Action

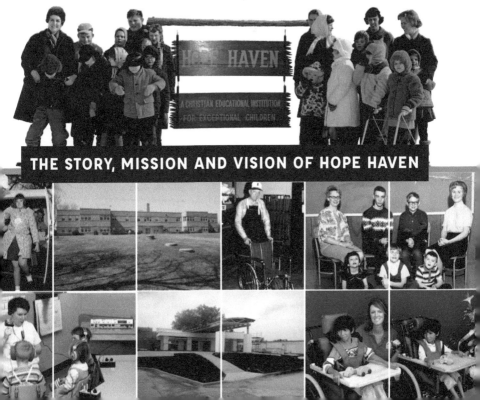

THE STORY, MISSION AND VISION OF HOPE HAVEN

Hope in Action

THE STORY, MISSION AND VISION OF HOPE HAVEN

THRONE
PUBLISHING GROUP

Printed in the United States of America.
Cover Design: Amy Gehling
Writer: Kelli Kissack, Certified StoryWay Guide
Copy Editor: Jessica Johnson, Certified StoryWay Guide
Proofing Editor: Certified StoryWay Guide

Throne Publishing Group and StoryWay
212 S Main Ave, Suite 204B
Sioux Falls, SD 57104

ThronePG.com

TABLE OF CONTENTS

Introduction

Introduction

INTRODUCTION

Thank you for picking up this book and taking the time to delve into the story of Hope Haven. We're sharing the way God has used ordinary people to accomplish extraordinary things in hopes of bringing Him the glory He deserves. We also want to explain where we've come from, where we are now, and where we hope to go. Hope Haven was started by a few people noticing a need, gathering together, and asking the simple question, "What can we do to help?" Today, that question continues to guide our ministry. The needs change, but the call to care for one another and foster God-given potential in all people does not.

We're on a mission to serve a certain group of people. In every corner of the globe, there are people with disabilities who are not being cared for or encouraged to reach their highest potential. Through God's guidance and provision, we help meet those needs all around the world. Whether it's wheelchairs distributed in Romania or Community Living Services in Rock Valley, Iowa, the needs are vast at home and abroad. As we share this story, we invite you to consider how you might play a role in Hope Haven's future. Our story is a testimony that all good things start with a strong cup of coffee, so if the Lord has placed a calling on your heart to help people with disabilities, please know there's a place for you here. We'd love to meet you for coffee and a conversation.

CHAPTER 1

Coffee and Hope

1
COFFEE AND HOPE

Four men sat in a booth with their heads bent in earnest conversation. As they talked, their calloused hands jotted notes on the thin napkins provided by Warren's Cafe of Rock Valley, Iowa. The year was 1959 and the men, each a pillar of their small farming town, were gathered together to discuss an important subject. As John Van Zanten, Reverend Milton Doorenbos, Harold Van Otterloo, and Ted Ribbens sipped on cups of strong coffee, their conversation settled into the question of the day. "What can we do for the children in our area that have special needs?"

It's a dangerous question. "What can *we* do?" Far different than saying, "Somebody else should do something," it opens the door to all kinds of wild ways that God can enter in and go to work, both in our hearts and in the world. Hope Haven's story begins with this simple question: What can we do?

In their own way, each man was well-acquainted with the realities of life for children with disabilities. John Van Zanten's two nephews were born with muscular dystrophy. He and his wife Mary knew two young children in their church who had severe hearing impairments. They also knew a young woman whose physical disabilities required her to be in a wheelchair.

In a rural area where most people attended a church within the Reformed denomination, Christian education was a high priority. In the late 1950s, the only Christian education available to children with disabilities was out-of-state. Sending a child to school meant not seeing them for six months at a time. While parents were welcome to visit, the 500-mile trip was too far for most families to make more than twice a year.

The parents who kept their children close to home and educated them in a traditional school encountered a different set of challenges. Most schools of the day, public or private, didn't have a special education teacher properly trained to help children with disabilities. There was also the issue of isolation. The common social view of the era was that if a child was born with a disability, their parents had surely committed some kind of grave sin to bring such shame on the family. People with disabilities were often isolated at home, rarely taken to town for shopping trips or even to church. If they were to go out, avoidance and wary glances were the usual response.

This was the reality that the four men meeting in the cafe that day understood all too well. It's the reason they united to find a better way. As fathers of young children, they couldn't imagine the pain of being separated from their kids for such long periods of time. They also believed what the Bible said, human beings are created in the image of God, filled with potential and deserving of dignity and individual choices.

Instead of closing their eyes to the need around them, they felt led by the Lord to do something about it. That day, they resolved to look at starting a Christian school for children with disabilities in Rock Valley. Being practical businessmen, they started with research. The Reformed Churches of the area already financially supported the school in Chicago, known as Elim, and Children's Retreat, the school in Grand Rapids. As the coffee cups grew cool and the napkins filled with ideas, a plan began to form. A road trip east was in order. The visits to Elim and Children's Retreat would guide their next steps.

> ⓘ Charles Kooima, the originator of Kooima Manufacturing, played an important role in the story of Hope Haven's founding. In addition to being the employer of 3 of the 4 men who gathered at Warren's Cafe, he was also the grandfather of John Van Zanten's two nephews who had muscular dystrophy. He encouraged the Hope Haven forefathers to pursue this cause and was generous with time off of work when they traveled to Elim and Children's Retreat. Charles also gave Ted Ribbens ample time off to canvas the churches and build the Hope Haven Society.

As the men gathered their belongings and stood to shake hands, they exchanged purposeful looks. The need was real, and they were going to do something about it. Of this much, they were sure. The future was uncertain, but in their hearts, a still, small voice moved, beckoning them to obey the calling placed on their lives. In the words of John Van Zanten, "When the Lord opens a door, you don't question it. You just walk through it."

A ROAD TRIP AND RESEARCH

The drive to Elim was full of anticipation. What would the school look like? How many students did it serve? Where did they find their staff? According to John Van Zanten, the group admired the services offered at Children's Retreat, but it was the visit to Elim that made the deepest impression on them. If they were to start something back home, this was the place they would model.

Elim served just under a hundred school-age students, and the place ran like a well-oiled machine. The staff was friendly and professional, the class schedule was consistent, and the adult work program was well underway. They even had a pool. The sheer impressiveness of it all made them wonder if something like it was possible in Rock Valley. The forefathers' competitive spirit was quickly roused when the staff at Elim heard of their intentions and responded with, "It's nice that you want to help, but it'll never work in the cornfields of Iowa." Despite this lackluster feedback, they were not dissuaded. On the trip home, the men visited about all they'd seen and agreed it was time to take the next step forward.

There was a known need, but how big was it? Were there enough children with disabilities to justify starting a school? To find answers to these questions, they needed to involve the area churches. By this point, Reverend Milton had relocated out of Rock Valley, so the remaining forefathers were John Van Zanten, Ted Ribbens, and Harold Van Otterloo. A letter was sent to all Reformed churches within a fifty-mile radius of Rock Valley, inviting the families who had children with disabilities to come together. Reaching out in faith, the forefathers set the date for August 12, 1960 at

Western Christian High School in Hull, Iowa. Their prayers were answered when over *fifty* children and their families came to the gathering. It was an eye-opening day for everyone involved. Several area pastors showed up and were surprised to learn that families they'd been shepherding for years had children with disabilities they'd never met. It was the first time that this many families in the area came together to celebrate their children with special needs.

The relief was palpable among the parents. Finally, they had a community where they could relate with other families who shared their concerns and joys. The possibility of a school in Rock Valley gave them hope that their children could get special education while remaining close to home. To John, Harold, and Ted, it was all the confirmation they needed. Their conclusion: "The Lord is opening a door. Now we must walk through it."

MISSION, VISION, AND FAITH

Hope Haven was the only name ever considered for the school because it clearly communicated its mission and purpose. In a time when there wasn't a lot of "Hope" for parents of children with disabilities, the school offered an opportunity for their children to reach their highest potential. "Haven" because it was a safe, Christian environment in which to learn and develop. A joyful, accepting place for those who often felt different and alone. A rainbow was incorporated into the logo because rather than gold at the end of the rainbow, there was hope, infinitely more valuable than any precious metal.

Together, these words clearly described the purpose of the school. It was to be a hopeful haven to all who came there, a welcoming place for everyone to realize their potential and be celebrated for their God-given value. The founders of Hope Haven wanted to do two things. First, help children with mental and physical disabilities and second, communicate God's love and train them in the Christian faith. To clearly define these values, they wrote a Statement of Philosophy and a Statement of Purpose.

Statement of Philosophy
"Services to people with disabilities at Hope Haven is considered a ministry of mercy based on the conviction that God's Word speaks to and directs all of life. That Word proclaims the healing ministry of Christ's command to love and show mercy to one another."

Statement of Purpose
"The purpose of Hope Haven is to assist people with disabilities to reach their potential...Hope Haven's major therapeutic tool is work...Hope Haven is a ministry of Christian training and mercy."

These original statements share the heart of the organization beautifully. A conviction is defined as "a firmly held belief," and the founding convictions of Hope Haven are simple. All people matter because they are created in the image and likeness of God. God directs all of life, and therefore people who have disabilities are just as full of intrinsic potential and purpose as someone who does not have a disability. The major tool used by Hope Haven to cultivate this potential is work, because work is a blessing from

God. He created human beings to work with purpose and intent, and this work brings dignity, individuality, and a sense of self-worth. This is a ministry of training, and training hints at an eventual graduation. The major goal of all of Hope Haven's services is to cultivate potential, equip clients with skills, and help them find their place as a contributing member of society. From the original statement of Philosophy and Purpose come the current mission and vision statements.

Mission Statement
"As followers of Christ, we unleash potential in people through work and life skills so that they may enjoy a productive life in their community."

Vision Statement
"Hope Haven is community committed to the special creation of God that is the human being; encouraging the realization of dreams, desires, and aspirations; valuing gifts, talents, and contributions; sharing accountability for individual and community growth."

Hope Haven was founded as a society rather than a church school because children from all denominational and faith backgrounds were welcome to attend. Founded on the basic belief that "these are God's children too," the Hope Haven school challenged society's view towards people with disabilities.

The underlying belief is that we have a responsibility to take care of others, not just ourselves. God gives each of us a clear commission to "love thy neighbor as thyself." That doesn't just apply to the people who look and act like us. These were the basic beliefs that propelled the founders into action and inspired the community to come alongside the mission. They were determined to be obedient to the Lord's calling and trusted that if they stepped out in faith, He would provide.

Organization and A Haven

2

ORGANIZATION AND A HAVEN

The first recorded Hope Haven committee meeting took place on February 6, 1960, about seven months prior to the Church Gathering Day. On August 19, 1960, the Hope Haven Society was officially formed and seven men were empowered to draft a constitution. In December of 1961, the first official society meeting was held and a constitution was accepted. Articles of Incorporation were approved and twenty-one men were elected to the Board of Trustees. A seven-member executive board was also voted upon, and their role was to oversee the school operations, manage the finances, hire the teachers, and find an administrator. The first Board of Trustees meeting, held on December 29, 1961, lasted several hours and covered an array of topics. When would school begin? How would they find the right teachers? Where would school be held? How would Hope Haven be funded? There were many details to work out, but the determined group of farmers and businessmen were efficient problem solvers. They operated with the certainty that the Lord was leading their steps and lighting their path. An idea which began over four cups of coffee and notes scribbled on napkins was becoming quite official, and even then, in the cornfields of Iowa, something great was beginning to take root and grow.

Rock Valley was chosen as the home of Hope Haven for a few reasons. First, it was the hometown of several of the founders. Second, there were talks of a building being donated for the school's use. While the donation never materialized, those factors cemented Rock Valley as the school's location. Around this time, the first deposits were made into the school's bank account. The first deposit was recorded as $25, and the first Treasurer's report recorded a total of $651.55 in the bank on February 7, 1962.

The first official Hope Haven parent meeting was held in June of 1960 at the First Christian Reformed Church in Rock Valley. The questions flew as fast as the founders could field them. Where would the teachers come from? Would those teachers have the right training? Where would the children stay who lived too far away to commute daily? How much would school tuition cost? What were the transportation arrangements? How long would the school year be?

The Hope Haven board members shared that tuition would be $15 per month with an enrollment fee of $20. However, the school's average expense to educate a student for one year was roughly $1600, so the difference would be made up in charitable donations. Overall, Hope Haven's first annual budget was $19,000.

The parents were excited but also hesitant. They knew their children needed special training, but because the school was a new venture, they were relying solely on the word and good faith of the board. Before that night, they had three options for their children's education: (1) send them to a traditional school that did not have a special education program, (2) send them all the way to Elim or Children's Retreat and not see them for six months of the year, or (3) keep them home and don't send them to school at all.

After hours of discussion, several families said, "We want to send our children to Hope Haven eventually, but why don't you get started this first year and we'll come the second year." An elderly gentleman stood up and said, "No, we can't do that. These people are trying to help our children and will do the best they can for them. We have to send our children now, so the school can get started." After his speech, there were no dry eyes in the church. Many parents committed to sending their children to Hope Haven that very night.

In June of 1962, the Hope Haven Society held a special meeting to discuss their goal of opening the school that fall. They needed to hire teachers, find a suitable space for classes to be held, and determine membership. They looked at several different locations, and even considered a former funeral home as an option. When they weren't able to secure a spot to hold school, plans were put on hold until the following year.

In 1963, the society tried again, but they couldn't secure the right teachers. The teachers who wanted to come to Rock Valley couldn't get out of their contracts at other schools, so the opening was once again delayed. On April 20, 1964, the board officially voted to utilize two rented classrooms at the Rock Valley Christian School. They acted on hiring Mrs. Prideaux for the hearing impaired students at a salary of $5500 per year. They hired Mrs. Hockman as the teacher for the students with physical and mental disabilities at a salary of $4000 per year. All of the pieces were finally falling into place for Hope Haven to officially open its doors.

THE FIRST DAY

On the morning of September 11, 1964, Hope Haven's board members, teachers, and students awoke feeling excited and, understandably, a little nervous. It was the first day of school. The preparations for this moment were years in the making, and everyone was eager to get started. The classrooms were ready, school supplies were in place, and each teacher stood waiting at the door to greet their new pupils as they arrived. John Van Zanten and a few other board members were also there, welcoming students and their families. A total of eleven children, ages five to eleven years old, attended Hope Haven the first year. The board hired well, and it was evident both teachers felt as called to the school as the board did. Everyone involved worked together to make it a safe, welcoming place to learn.

The first day at Hope Haven symbolized much more than the start of a new school year. For so many parents, it was a beacon of hope that their children would receive a Christian education tailored specifically to their needs. It also meant they could reach their highest potential without being 500 miles away. For the students, it was a haven of safety, acceptance, and similarity. Growing up in a culture where they often felt isolated and different, Hope Haven was the place where they could just be children, like anyone else. Yet the Lord had much, much more in store for the fledgling ministry. What began with two teachers, two small classrooms, and eleven students was about to grow exponentially, faster than anyone imagined possible.

A DECADE OF FIRSTS

The sixties were filled with exciting milestones and "firsts" for Hope Haven. Years of prayer, research, planning, and preparation culminated in the successful opening of the Hope Haven school in 1964. The following year, enrollment blossomed to twenty-seven students after the Christian Hope Center in the nearby town of Sioux Center agreed to merge with Hope Haven. The rapid growth prompted the board to rent a stand-alone building from the Rock Valley Christian School. They made another landmark decision when they moved to hire Harvey De Jager as Hope Haven's first executive director in January of 1965.

The year of 1966 brought more expansion. The school that wasn't supposed to grow in the cornfields of Iowa was blossoming. Enrollment boomed to thirty-six students. The former Methodist Church building was rented for extra classroom space. The need for Hope Haven to have its own, stand-alone building was becoming obvious. There was a waiting list of students who wanted to come to school, but without additional space, there simply wasn't room.

In January of 1966, the board approved the proposal for the construction of Hope Haven's first building. Step one was purchasing a small piece of land from Rock Valley Cement and Gravel. At the time, the land was being used as a sandpit, but Fred De Jong Excavation generously volunteered to fill it in, free of charge, so that the building project could proceed. A local family donated just over three acres, and Hope Haven purchased a few smaller tracts from the city and other private parties to bring the total size to 12.33 acres.

Step two was raising money for construction of the $360,000 project. The Hope Haven board selected two members from each congregation that belonged to the Society to head up the fundraising efforts in their church. Harvey De Jager also played a key role in raising funds for the building. Harvey's official title was executive director, but he wore many hats including that of administrator and fundraiser. Through the Lord's provision, half of the construction budget was raised before building began in the fall of 1966. On September 27, 1967, they celebrated the grand opening and dedication of Hope Haven's first building. Outfitted with eight classrooms, a gym, a dining room, and a living center, it was specifically designed to meet the needs of the growing school. In its first year of operation, the new building served over fifty enrolled students.

The exciting growth of Hope Haven's student body meant that several children were coming from areas beyond commuting distance to Rock Valley. Because traveling back-and-forth daily was not feasible, they needed safe homes near town where they could stay during the week. The Hope Haven Society asked members of local churches to serve as foster families. They were paid to house the students, however, the Lord worked through this program to transform many hearts in Rock Valley. Instead of keeping their distance, families learned to see children with disabilities as God's children. Valued, loved and full of potential. A town transformation occurred one home at a time.

In the late 1960s, many of the students who came from the Christian Hope Center "aged out" of Hope Haven's educational programs. At the time, the Iowa Legislature provided educational funding until the age of twenty-one. Many of the Christian Hope Center students were in their late-teens when they transferred to Hope Haven, and when they turned twenty-one, they could no longer attend school.

This was a problem because the employment and life skills training opportunities for adults with disabilities were slim to none. They either continued to live with their parents or went to live at "county farms," which were county-owned facilities for people with disabilities. They offered little in the way of work skills or individual choices.

It didn't take long for the Hope Haven Society to recognize the need for work and life skills training among the graduating adults. Through John Van Zanten's background in manufacturing, the Hope Haven Work Training Program began with a few former students assembling parts for Kooima Manufacturing. The basement was the only place that had enough room for the manufacturing tools, so that's where the Work Training Program began. The goal was simple: offer people with disabilities dignity through real work and real wages. The assembly jobs included adding metal loops to hitch pins and fitting rubber parts to valve stems and automotive solenoids.

CLIENT STORY: MARCIA DE JONG

Marcia De Jong was born on June 11, 1955, the daughter of Fred and Jean De Jong. The De Jongs had six children, and when it was time for Marcia, their third child, to go to school the options were limited because of her mental disability and serious visual impairment. The family doctor offered little hope for Marcia's future and encouraged her parents to "put her away in an institution." Like most parents, they had little knowledge of the "state home" so their visit was a shock.

"She was still quite young then. We walked around the facility and it just made me sick. I would never put her in such a place!" said Marcia's father, Fred.

The De Jongs continued to search for a better option. When Hope Haven was established in 1964, their prayers were answered and 9-year-old Marcia enrolled in the inaugural class. Thanks to visionary leaders, loving staff, committed volunteers, and many generous donors, the school was the first of many of Hope Haven's ministries to enrich the lives of people who once had few options.

After Marcia completed her schooling, she enrolled in Hope Haven's first work training programs. She became a model employee at two work sites, and her life was enriched by her growing independence and success at multiple jobs. She worked hard and was proud of her income.

Marcia lived at home in Hull, Iowa with her parents until she moved to Hope Haven's group home, Northside Court, also located in Hull. She was 36-years-old, and Fred and Jean were grateful that Hope Haven opened a residential program in their hometown.

"Hope Haven was a wonderful answer to prayer," Jean recalled. "As a mom, I wanted to do things for her, but at Hope Haven, they taught her to do for herself. It was amazing to see what she was able to accomplish through training."

"Even with limited vision, Marcia liked to be as independent as possible. She washed her dishes and did her own laundry. She even cooked,"

said Marcia's Residential Specialist. "Marcia's enthusiasm for work was remarkable. We could all learn from her!"

Marcia loved to send cards for the birthdays and anniversaries of her family members, friends, and church members. If anyone was struggling, she was the first person to say, "We have to pray for them." She often became emotional because she cared so much.

Marcia was a "people person" who loved visiting the public library and picking out new books to read. She enjoyed eating out with friends and had a terrific sense of humor. For years she participated in the Special Olympics with a large family section cheering her on in every event.

The highlight of Marcia's life was her profession of faith. Through Friendship Bible Studies, a program that offered one-on-one teaching of Bible truths to people with disabilities, she gained a new and deeper understanding of the Gospel. Marcia passed away in November of 2016, and she is dearly missed by the staff at Hope Haven. Her smile, contagious enthusiasm, and caring heart left an unerasable mark on us all.

If we would have looked into the basement of Hope Haven as the work training program was beginning, we would have witnessed eight to ten people working on various projects. A bandsaw, a drill press, and a few other manufacturing tools would have been placed in different parts of the 1500 square foot basement, racks of steel bars stacked on the far side of the room. Clients learned the five to six steps necessary to operate their piece of equipment. They were also taught how to check the quality of their work. Paid on the basis of production, they earned the exact same prorated wage as the employees doing similar jobs at the Kooima Manufacturing building.

The ultimate goal of the program was to graduate clients from the training program into a job in the community.

At this time, providing Christian education to children with disabilities was a whole new concept. Therefore, teaching adults with disabilities to have work and life skills, especially in manufacturing, was even more "out there." There was some minor pushback from the community, but in time, the doubts faded away. The quality work, excellent safety record, and high job placement began to speak for themselves.

The origins of the Work Training Program tie directly back to Hope Haven's founding purpose statement. Helping people with disabilities reach their full potential and find dignity through work as a therapeutic tool. In the heart of every human being is the desire to find purpose through work. Work provides income, which in turn, offers options, choices, and the chance for individuality. The mission of Hope Haven is not to create a sub-culture among people with disabilities, but rather to see the community embrace each person, disabled or not, as a person with something to offer society. The intrinsic truth behind the Work Training Program is that they belong to God, just like us. They have abilities and potential. They are not limited by society's perceptions or beliefs about them.

The Work Training Program was tested on a small scale and when it showed promise, it was expanded to help more people. This is the way Hope Haven has developed each of its programs. See a need, find a solution, test the solution. If it works, make it bigger.

By the end of the 1960s, Hope Haven seemed unstoppable. The school was thriving in a brand new building. The Work Training

Program grew so quickly that in 1969, it moved out of the basement and into a building on Main Street. Students were learning, clients were growing, and the community was embracing people with disabilities. The churches were supportive. Things couldn't have been better. The foundations of Hope Haven seemed unshakeable, but no one could have imagined the trials that were to come.

Formation Through Challenges

3

FORMATION THROUGH CHALLENGES

UNSTOPPABLE MOMENTUM

Rolling into the 1970s, Hope Haven seemed to be an unstoppable force. School enrollment was growing rapidly. Group homes were being established because so many children were coming to school from outside of the area. The adult programs were also booming. In early 1971, Hope Haven completed construction of a dedicated workshop for adult services and work training programs which served around forty-eight adults.

In 1972, Hope Haven began two more building projects. The first was an addition onto the original Hope Haven building. This wing became the Child Development Center, a therapy facility for children with severe and demanding physical needs. The second project was a larger building for the Work Training Program because it outgrew its new facility in less than a year.

By 1973, Hope Haven served approximately 240 children and adults through its various programs. It was known as *the place* for people with disabilities to blossom to their full potential. The society of churches was engaged and supportive, fully invested in the ministry's mission and vision. An example of this community support was the "green stamp drive," a society-led fundraising effort that encouraged people to save their S&H green stamps and donate them to Hope Haven. Green stamps were a line of trading stamps put out by the Sperry & Hutchinson Company. The stamps could be collected, put into a stamp booklet, and redeemed for rewards in the S&H catalog. The community responded with so much enthusiasm that Hope Haven was able to purchase two passenger vans solely through the stamps.

From 1965 to 1973, Hope Haven completed three major building projects and grew to offer all the services a child with special needs may require, including Christian education, full-service physical and speech therapy, and residential services like group home housing. With students coming from as far away as Manhattan, Montana, residential services became an important part of the ministry. The school's growth exceeded anything the forefathers had imagined. In less than a decade, Hope Haven grew to be twice the size of Elim, the Chicago school that inspired the founders in the first place. The confidence of the community, the parents, and the students was high. Hope Haven didn't just offer school, or work, or residential services, it offered everything.

As the ministry's reputation grew, it began to attract even more talented, vocationally-minded staff members. There are stories of people who completely changed their college major so they could apply at Hope Haven after graduation. It was a ministry-minded, church-supported place that had a great reputation. People wanted to be a part of the team. This attraction of talent was one of the reasons Hope Haven could grow so quickly. The staff knew the mission, purpose, and philosophy of the organization, and when they showed up for work, they hit the ground running. It seemed like nothing could stop the momentum. That was before events at the State Legislature changed the ministry forever.

STRENGTH THROUGH CHALLENGE

Life happens in cycles similar to the way the earth works in seasons. At the dawn of 1974, Hope Haven entered a cycle of challenge and refinement. After the booming growth of the sixties and early seventies, this season of challenge was the last thing they saw coming. That's because the change began a long way away from the sleepy town of Rock Valley, in Iowa's state capital of Des Moines.

In 1974, the Iowa state government reorganized the jurisdiction of the state government agency that was responsible for the education of people with special needs. This was impactful to Hope Haven for a few reasons. The first related to funding.

At Hope Haven, each student or adult client who receives services comes to the organization with multiple funding streams. Similar to the way a college student pays for their tuition with a mixture of scholarships, loans, and grants, a student or adult client comes to Hope Haven with multiple streams of funding to support them. Prior to 1974, the most common funding stream was financial support from the state of Iowa. This all changed when Iowa re-departmentalized and moved jurisdiction over the education of people with special needs from the Department of Social Services to the

Department of Public Education. Since the beginning of Hope Haven's ministry, the Department of Social Services was supportive of its mission as a Christ-centered organization. When jurisdiction was transferred to the Department of Public Education, they basically said, "We can't continue funding you unless you switch to a secular curriculum." Suddenly Hope Haven found itself at a fork in the road. There were two options: (1) change the curriculum to a secular-based program and continue to receive funding from the state, or (2) continue on as a Biblically-based school providing Christian education and lose their main funding source. Caught between a rock and a hard place, the way forward didn't seem clear.

The decision was further complicated by the fact that Hope Haven was founded as a "society," rather than a church school, and the society included congregations belonging to five different types of Reformed Churches. These five denominations had differing views on private versus public education. One denomination was against public education and vehemently opposed the idea of changing the curriculum. Other groups were supportive of public schooling and didn't see a problem with the Department of Education's ultimatum. The future of Hope Haven dangled in the balance.

Ultimately, the board voted to remain a Christian school with Biblically-based curriculum and gave up the public funding. Instead, they would attempt to run the school strictly on charitable contributions. It turned out to be a disaster. The 1974 conflict left the society so fractured that charitable giving and church financial support dropped to an all-time low. Many of the denominations that favored public education refused to support Hope Haven financially because they didn't see why Hope Haven needed their money. "If they'd simply change the curriculum, all their problems would be solved." This was the viewpoint of some churches in the society. Other churches supported the decision to remain a Biblically-based school, but their financial gifts weren't enough to meet Hope Haven's growing budget.

By 1976, the ministry was in such a poor financial position that the bank refused to loan them any more money. It was the lowest point in Hope Haven's history. Staff members weren't getting their paychecks and tensions were high. Many staff members wondered if they needed to find a new job. When the bank said, "No more" and that funding stream disappeared, it seemed there was nothing left to do but close the doors. However, God is faithful in continuing the work He began. At the last moment, an anonymous group of private investors went to the bank and offered to co-sign Hope Haven's loan to keep the doors open and ensure the staff got paid. They provided the immediate money needed to keep the ministry afloat, but it came with a condition. It was time to face the facts about the school. In order to keep Hope Haven alive, the educational process needed to change. In 1978, the board once again took a vote, deciding this time to turn the Hope Haven school over to Area Four of Iowa's Department of Public Education.

This is where the story becomes even more interesting. Looking at transition from inside the school's walls, not all that much changed for the students and teachers. The former Hope Haven School became known as River Valley School. Area Four brought in a new principal but rented all of Hope Haven's classrooms and hired all the existing teachers. Serving the students became a joint effort as Area Four was responsible for their education and Hope Haven provided for their physical needs such as therapy services and housing.

Externally, the change was more dramatic. It turned out to be a big deal. A really big deal. After the decision was made to turn the school over to the state, a public forum was held in Rock Valley to discuss what the change meant for Hope Haven's future. Churches from all over Minnesota, South Dakota, and Iowa chartered coach buses to bring their members to this meeting. One Hope Haven staff member described the atmosphere as intense, angry, and riotous. Some members of the society were adamantly against the change and viewed it as "selling out" or "selling Hope Haven's birthright." Other members wanted it and thought it would fix the ministry's financial woes. Anger and passion surrounded this change because it hinged on two of the most divisive subjects known to humanity: religion and politics. The denominational differences, as inconsequential as they seem today, felt insurmountable at the time. There was also a strong resistance to the idea of becoming "government controlled." Many people didn't trust government oversight, so the idea of Hope Haven School coming under the state government's jurisdiction was ghastly to them.

Members of the board endured a lot of criticism during this time. The conflict became so severe that some of them suffered loss of their personal property. An arsonist set twenty fires in the Rock Valley area throughout the years of 1975 to 1977. John Van Zanten's barn, a Hope Haven executive's home, and a Christian Reformed Church were all victims of arson. While the culprit was never caught and a direct link never proven, many in the community wanted to connect the crimes to Hope Haven's situation. Deep hurt and anger fractured the once unified society that propelled Hope Haven. The strong community support was gone, yet God's calling to serve people with disabilities was still there. Unsure of its future, Hope Haven needed to find a new way forward.

THE JOURNEY TO HEALING

The deep scars, hostility, and anger remained long after the educational shake-up of 1974. The journey to hope and healing was not an easy one. When the church society no longer supported Hope Haven, a new group stepped up to meet the practical needs of the school. In February of 1977, the Hope Haven Christian Women's Auxiliary was established with the purpose of raising money to meet the everyday needs of the school. Their example showed the way toward forgiveness, healing, and reconciliation.

An auxiliary is a support group, similar to a booster club, that raises funds to meet the needs of an organization. Open to any woman, including those outside of the Reformed persuasion, who wanted to support the mission and purpose of Hope Haven, the group's membership was around 150 women. They recognized that the original funding sources had dried up, so they began collecting Campbell's soup labels, hosting silent auctions, and selling food and crafts at local county fairs in order to raise money. With a true mothering spirit, the group supplied things like basketballs for the Special Olympics and new kitchen equipment for the hot lunch program. Their heartfelt efforts slowly began bringing the community back to the center of Hope Haven's vision. The Women's Auxiliary helped to break down denominational barriers and rally the Christian community around the mission of Hope Haven. They provided steady, consistent support and raised funds for smaller scale purchases that met the practical needs of Hope Haven's children. Slowly but surely, glimmers of healing began to appear on the horizon.

As the sources of support and funding changed, so did the scope of Hope Haven's students and clients. During the reorganization in Des Moines, the Department of Education issued a mandate that every school district was responsible for the education of every child in their district. Before the mandate, Hope Haven was getting students from every part of Iowa since most schools didn't have special education teachers. At its peak, Hope Haven School served between 130-140 students, with 78 foster homes and 12 group homes hosting students residentially.

After the state's reorganization, most of the public schools began hiring their own special education teachers, and when that happened, several students were mainstreamed back into their local school systems. This caused many of Hope Haven's children's group homes to be closed. Also, less foster homes were needed. After this happened and Hope Haven School became River Valley School, enrollment decreased to about eighty students, with only twelve to eighteen children served residentially. Many of the students who remained, had disabilities so severe that they needed full-time care and therapy services in a group home setting. Essentially, Hope Haven's children's services shrunk to almost nothing because the need for residential services changed so dramatically after the state reorganization. Even though these circumstances were out of the ministry's control, Hope Haven was challenged to adjust, pivot, and evolve.

Evolve is exactly what Hope Haven did. Even though the school program changed and children's services shrank drastically, the adult programs were blossoming. In 1973, they were reorganized into two groups: the skills-intensive Work Training Program and a more sheltered workshop setting, known as the Work Activities Center.

Another milestone innovation of the 1970s was the launch of the Horizons newsletter, an important communication tool that went out four times per year. As the wounds of the mid-seventies continued to heal, it was important to keep the doors of communication open and inviting, and Horizons was a major initiative to do just that. The quarterly missive was filled with stories of Hope Haven clients, interesting bits of ministry news, and a list of upcoming events and activities. The mission of Hope Haven was on full display as stories of clients learning new skills, gaining employment in the community, and having new adventures filled the pages of that first issue.

CLIENT STORY: EMLYN DE STIGTER

Leonard and Ella De Stigter of Sioux Center, Iowa, wanted the same things for their daughter Emlyn, who was born with Down's Syndrome, as they wanted for their other children. In 1953, there were no programs in the region to offer support to her family or educational services to "Emy."

Doctors told Leonard and Ella that Emy couldn't do much and probably wouldn't live beyond the age of 15. They did what they could at home, but what they wanted most was an education for their daughter. Kind neighbors were wonderfully supportive and helped teach Emy, but she still needed to go to school. When Hope Haven launched its ministry in 1964, 10-year-old Emy was part of the first class. For the first time, the De Stigters had hope that their daughter would get an education.

"What made Hope Haven special is the way it brought people out into the community so those with disabilities weren't hidden anymore. We heard of families that hid their children so no one knew they existed. Thanks to Hope Haven, people with special needs were brought into the community and the church," Leonard explained.

When Emy finished her schooling, she joined the work training program. She was employed through Hope Haven's programs from 1974 to 2009, receiving training and support in varied settings and for many tasks. She worked full-time for many years packaging candy, assembling muffler clamps, making boxes, and crafting rubber mats. Emy was grateful for work and celebrated the fact that "the more she worked the more she earned."

Emy lived at home with her parents in Sioux Center until she was 36-years-old, when she moved to Northside Court in Hull, Iowa. Her parents were impressed by the new skills Emy acquired and were appreciative of the loving staff who helped her gain independence. The residential specialists taught her banking, shopping, cooking, laundry, and cleaning skills. In 1993, Emy moved to a new residential community in Sioux Center called Ridgebrook Apartments. She was happy to move closer to family, but she always described her own cozy apartment as her home.

Emy passed away in January of 2009 at the age of sixty-one. She was spending the night at her parents' home for the New Year's holiday. When her mother joined Emy for bedtime prayers, she was blessed

to hear her daughter's final words, a favorite prayer since childhood:
"If I should die before I wake, I pray the Lord my soul to keep."

In spite of the turbulence of the mid-seventies, Hope Haven continued to look for open doors to meet the needs of people with disabilities. As the ministry forged new frontiers in work services, they shared their knowledge with young, fledgling organizations to help them get their start. With the goal of getting as many adults back into their home communities as possible, equipping these new organizations gave Hope Haven an opportunity to bring others into the new frontier of work services for people with disabilities. These workshops sprouted across Iowa in Sheldon, Le Mars, and Onawa plus a location in Sioux Falls, South Dakota. The plan to support and encourage these organizations until they became financially independent was a success. All of them are still in operation today, faithfully meeting the needs of the people in their communities.

During this decade, Hope Haven endured some of the most difficult, refining challenges of its existence. From the astonishing growth of the sixties and early seventies to the lowest lows of the mid-seventies, Hope Haven grew in strength, resilience and grit as it emerged from the literal fires of change. Yet in the most difficult circumstances, the ministry continued to live out its mission of unleashing potential in people with disabilities. It did this by expanding the adult programs, founding the satellite work training workshops, and continuing to serve the children in its group homes and therapy services. Despite the external conflict and lack of community support, Hope Haven never wavered from God's calling. This rock-solid faith in God's call and the determination to keep going is what kept the doors of Hope Haven open throughout the darkest years. It is also what propelled the organization into the years of growth and multiplication that awaited them in the booming times of the eighties.

HOPE HAVEN

Memories through the Years

**1964 | First Hope Haven
Board of Trustees**

1965 | School

1966 | First Building Committee

1967 | Drawing of the
Hope Haven building

First Hope Haven School Bus

**Beginning Class of the
Hope Haven School**

One of the first students Emlyn De Stigter

**Early
Classroom Photo**

1967 | School Building Construction

1970 | Work Activity Center

1972 | Adding Wing to Building for Work Activity

1976 | First home for residents.
George Veenendahl sitting on the steps.

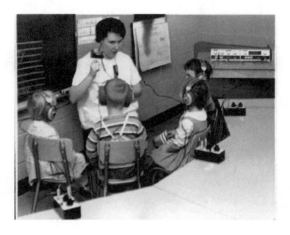

Deaf Children Learning in the Classroom

Early working in Work Training Center

Hope Haven Christian Women's Auxiliary purchased this
16mm movie projector with soup labels

Hope Haven Christian Women's Auxiliary sorting
Campbell's Soup Labels

Holland House - Verna Haverhals

One of the First Class Photos Taken

**Early class picture |
Marcia De Jong is front row, middle student**

1977 | Women's Auxiliary Started

1981 | RTC Building | First time management of a county facility turned over to a private agency, Hope Haven

Marcia De Jong at Special Olympics

**Founded in 1989 | Early Hope Haven Support
Foundation Board of Directors**

1989 | Niessink Fire

1991 | The first Intermediate Care Facility Homes: Westview Homes

1994 | HHIM Volunteers Begin

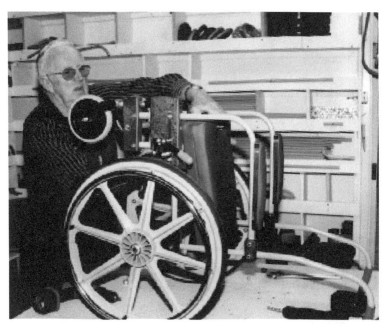

Volunteers | Jr Reinders Working on a Wheelchair at the
Ireton Wheelchair Ministry Center

Work Training Center in Basement

First Group Home in Pipestone, MN

Overall View of Double HH Manufacturing

1998 | Double HH Manufacturing
Moves into New Building

**2001 | Some of the First KidChairs
Designed and Distributed**

**Double HH Manufacturing Sign
Outside of New Location**

2008 | HHIM Opens New
Workshop in Guatemala

Double HH Manufacturing Designs New Hitch Pin -
Lockease Safety Hitch Pin

Campaign to Remodel Main Building

**June 2014 | Flood Which Displaced Those
Living at Westview Homes**

**2018 | New Brand and
Logo Implemented**

2020 | Rock Valley Home

CHAPTER 4

Restoration and Growth

GROWTH IN SIOUX COUNTY

After the literal and figurative fires of the seventies, everyone at Hope Haven was eager for a new decade full of life and restored hope. The ministry survived the most trying times of its existence, and now it was time to face an uncertain future. Without a school, what was the basis of Hope Haven? Where would it grow from here? Where is the Lord leading us? The answer came in the form of another open door, right in Sioux County. The way Hope Haven walked through this door set the tone for the rest of the decade.

On March 2, 1981, Hope Haven took over management of the Sioux County Care Facility, sometimes also referred to as "the county farm." Before Hope Haven existed, the county care facility was one of the only residential options for adults with disabilities. The residents' needs were met, but in more of a "ward" style of administration. The residents enjoyed very little individuality. They lived in dormitory style rooms, couldn't choose the type of toothpaste they wanted to use, the TV show they wanted to watch, or the kind of clothes they wanted to wear.

Prior to 1981, a few adults from this facility were attending Hope Haven for work training, but the staff realized they couldn't fully blossom because they lived within this standardized system of management. The Hope Haven leadership realized they could save the county money by managing the program while also helping the residents live better lives. Another pioneering effort, this was the first time the management of a county facility was taken over by a private entity.

As Hope Haven executed this management change, they brought in their own administrative team and worked to move the rest of the facility's original staff from a "ward" concept to the mindset of creating an integrative life for the residents. There were about sixty people living at the care facility at the time. The main goal was to increase the number of people engaging in the work training programs while also cultivating individuality and personal dignity amongst the residents.

Moving residents into individual rooms, cultivating their personal preferences, and engaging more people in the Work Training Program meant that within just a few years, the number of residents living there decreased from sixty to thirty-five. This was a huge success because Hope Haven is a community-based organization with the ultimate goal of helping each person achieve their full potential. Many of the people living at the Sioux County Care Facility had the potential to live quite independently but had never gotten the life or work skills training to do so. If their full potential meant they could live on their own and work in community-based employment, then that was the goal.

CLIENT STORY: GEORGE VEENENDAHL

Abandoned at a state institution as a newborn, George lived in lonely isolation with no record of a visitor in twenty-two years. Diagnosed with developmental disabilities and impaired vision, he had never been in a home, never visited a church, and had not learned basic skills for independent living. Hope Haven gave George a new life of hope when he moved into the foster home program in 1967. After growing up in a ward with 40 other boys, he had his own room in the Rock Valley home of Lloyd and Pearl Munneke.

He learned what belonged in the refrigerator and how to wash and dry dishes. He watched his first TV show and became an enthusiastic fan of area athletics. The Munnekes also taught him about Jesus and took him to church. Lloyd recalled giving George money for the offering the first time they took him to church. George was reluctant to part with his new cash. When he put it in the offering plate, he loudly asked, "Do we have to pay every time?"

"I didn't even know Jesus when I came to Hope Haven. It was the first time I heard about Jesus and that God created us in His own image and that Jesus died on the cross to take our sins away," George said.

He began attending services at Calvin Christian Reformed Church in Rock Valley.

Rev. John Engbers, the now-retired pastor of this church said, "I often wished everyone attended services as faithfully as George."

Pastor Engbers recalls that George chastised him for swearing while reading Scripture. Puzzled at first, Pastor Engbers respected George's confusion and changed his offensive word to "donkey." He chuckles when he explains that in the early years, George copied his pulpit greeting every time they met. With arms spread wide and voice booming, George proclaimed, "Beloved!" because it was the way the Pastor greeted the congregation from the pulpit. The retired pastor will never forget George's profession of faith and his baptism.

The elders asked, "Do you love Jesus?"

George passionately replied, "I sure do!"

Then they asked, "How do you know that there is a God?"

He replied, "Because He is in my heart, and I pray to Him every day!"

Pastor Engbers brought him to church the Saturday before his baptism so he would know what to expect. As he got down on his knees in front of the baptismal font, the pastor explained that he would place the waters of baptism on his head, and George exclaimed, "Ain't this something!"

A charter member of many Hope Haven employment services, he tied ropes for meat processing plants, packaged farm gate latches, and manufactured safety floor mats for U.S. military cars and tanks. George is now retired.

Changing the culture of a managed care facility is one thing. Changing the culture of a whole town is another. Orange City, Iowa was the nearest community, located just a mile down the road from the care facility. To help the residents develop life and work skills, Hope Haven staff began taking them to town, going to sporting events, church, doctors' appointments, shopping, and making purchases. To ease the nature of this transition, Hope Haven staff met with community leaders, churches, and businesses to share that things would be managed differently than before.

Prior to 1981, residents of the county facility were called "inmates" and a significant "us versus them" mentality framed the way people in Orange City viewed the residents. For example, when it was time for the annual Tulip Festival parade, residents from the county facility rode into town on a school bus to watch the festivities, but they weren't allowed to get off the bus. As the colorful floats and merry music marched by, the windows of the bus came down and heads peered out, taking in the sights from the boundary of the bus. After the management changes of 1981, those barriers disappeared and isolation was replaced with integration.

To build these new bridges in the community, Hope Haven staff members initially went to church with residents, took them shopping, went on supervised grocery trips, and other adventures into the community. Then, the supervision slowly phased out and volunteers within churches picked up residents for church or shopping trips. Next, a Big Brother Big Sister program was created so that residents had people to go with them to social activities. These big brothers and big sisters didn't just teach the residents skills, they truly took their hand and helped them understand how to operate in the community. They also modeled to the rest of the community how to come alongside people with disabilities in a way that makes them feel valued and worthy. Orange City was the first town, outside of Rock Valley, that went through this kind of heart transformation towards people with special needs.

Hope Haven is built on the belief that every life has a purpose, meaning, and importance. Every person deserves personal dignity and individual choices, and it's our responsibility to help them uncover those things. Yet because of the way God designed humanity to work, a person can't fully understand their purpose without living in a community. In turn, the community can't understand their purpose without knowing and recognizing the individuals that comprise it. Neither entity can be fully recognized or wholly functional without the other. This is the Divine symbiosis, created by God to help us recognize our need for one another. The residents of the county care facility needed help uncovering their unique gifts and realizing how they could contribute. This blessing of contribution is fertile ground in which personal pride and dignity takes root. Each person has the basic need for others to accept them and to recognize the role they play in the greater good of the community. The premise of Hope Haven's mission is that God is directing the lives of people with disabilities just as He's directing our lives.

HARVEY'S RETURN

In January of 1982, a second major milestone of the early eighties happened when Harvey De Jager, Hope Haven's first executive director, returned as CEO. After not operating within budget for several years, the ministry found itself in a precarious financial spot. The board asked Harvey if he would come back and get things back on track. A self-described "problem solver, not a maintainer," Harvey was just the person to help Hope Haven dig its way out of a large financial hole, but what they were asking was no small undertaking. He needed to trim the budget while maintaining the quality of the services provided to the clients, but if there was a leader who could do it, it was Harvey. His was distinct, autocratic, and refining.

Exactly the kind of CEO needed during a season of rebuilding.

Harvey knew his decisions wouldn't make him the most popular guy in town. He also knew the challenges ahead of the ministry, and in order to get back on track, he needed staff members with heart. Instead of asking for balance sheets or profit and loss statements, he started with a walk around Hope Haven. There was hard, non-glamorous, back-to-the-basics work ahead of them, and anyone giving a half-hearted effort simply couldn't remain on the payroll. He laid off fourteen staff members during the first week, and the response from the community was not kind. In a small town like Rock Valley, everyone is related to everyone else, and people stopped Harvey on the street, asking him why he laid off their uncle, or cousin, or sister. Explaining that tough choices were made so that Hope Haven would survive, he continued ahead and left all dreams of winning a popularity contest behind.

The first week back was difficult to say the least. Just a few days into his new (old) job, a notice came from the Department of Labor saying Hope Haven owed the government over $1 million in back wages. To make matters worse, the ministry's financial records were a mess, the bookkeeping was inaccurate, and the budget was not being followed. To turn the ship around and set the organization up for long term success, it was time to return to the fundamentals. A lean, agile staff, accurate bookkeeping, and high-quality client services that could be delivered within Hope Haven's annual budget. Tough decisions were made, all for the purpose of turning the ministry around, and turnaround it did. Within four years, Hope Haven erased over $600,000 in debt, grew the endowment, and increased agency equity to nearly $3 million.

Harvey's job was to correct a lot of things that weren't done correctly, to shore up operations, and strengthen Hope Haven's foundation as it recovered from the hardships of the seventies. Sometimes, this kind of leader isn't appreciated while the work is being done. Change like this is hard and it's painful, but it was necessary for Hope Haven's survival. Making these difficult changes set Hope Haven on a long-term track of restoration and growth that it had never experienced before.

MILESTONES AND MEANING

As Hope Haven regained its feet, the ministry continued to march forward by asking the same dangerous question. "What can we do?" Every time that question was asked, the Lord showed Hope Haven another open door. In 1983, an exciting new phase of the residential training programs began when Hope Haven made the decision to bring more oversight into its foster care program and move away from individualized, community-based foster homes. Prior to Harvey's return, Hope Haven had between seventy-five and eighty foster homes. The foster parents were great people, but there was very little oversight on them because there was no administrative head to manage the foster parents. To solve this challenge, Hope Haven built three Housing and Urban Development (HUD) homes and kicked off a brand new phase of residential training programs where more people lived in Hope Haven-managed group homes rather than individuals being placed with foster parents. This was an important step for the organization because it increased the amount of accountability, authority, and oversight within its residential programs.

In 1985, Hope Haven took another pioneering step by purchasing a restaurant in Sioux Center known as the Holland House. At that time, the economy wasn't very good and it was hard to find jobs for people with disabilities. Harvey knew of a restaurant in Ohio that employed people with special needs, so he pitched the idea of buying a restaurant to the Hope Haven board and they agreed. The goal was to use the Holland House as the launching pad of the new Community Based Employment (CBE) program. The majority of the ten staff that worked each shift were people with special needs. Seeing them clear tables, waitress, dishwash, and do maintenance work opened the eyes of the community to the fact that people with disabilities could be highly successful employees. Soon other restaurants like Pizza Ranch and the Supreme Egg began hiring Hope Haven clients to work in their businesses. The Holland House was instrumental in changing the community's perception of people with special needs and opening doors for more clients to find jobs in the community.

In the spring of 1986, Harvey announced that he was leaving. This wasn't a surprise because he'd told the board before he agreed to come back that it wouldn't be permanent. He got the ministry to a stable place and then it was time for a new leader to take over. In 1986, David VanNingen became the fifth executive director in Hope Haven's history. David and Harvey couldn't have been more different. Their personalities and leadership styles were opposite but they greatly respected one another. God has always been faithful to bring Hope Haven the right leader at the right time. David, in his quiet but powerful way, taught his team to be sensitive to the Lord's leading, to be eager, and to be adventurous. He modeled to them how to become comfortable with being uncomfortable. He was exactly the kind of leader Hope Haven needed as it prepared to enter several decades of growth.

That expansion began with the founding of a new mental health program in 1988. No one else in the state was offering this kind of program at the time. In fact, it was so new that Hope Haven sent two staff members to Boston University to get their Masters degrees in Psychiatric-Rehabilitation. The pioneering program served individuals with chronic mental health disabilities. Today it's known as Mental Health and Recovery Services.

Another pioneering effort of the decade was the establishment of the Religious Services program which began in the late 1980's. The purpose of this program was to integrate people with disabilities into community churches with the hope that they would begin embracing people with special needs into their congregations and services.

In 1989, Hope Haven celebrated its 25th year of ministry. This was also the year the Hope Haven Support Foundation was established. After the tumultuous years of the seventies and early eighties, the board and Hope Haven's senior leadership recognized the need to bring stability into its finances. The sole purpose of starting the foundation was to make the work of Hope Haven stable for the long-term. The initial goal was to raise and house one year's operating budget within the foundation. Thus, the Hope Haven Support Foundation was established and the fund raising efforts began. Joe Van Tol served as the first foundation board president and still serves in that capacity today. It's interesting that when the foundation began, its sole purpose was to fund the work of Hope Haven in a tri-state region. What the leaders of Hope Haven didn't know is that God had a much, much larger geographical area in mind for their foundation dollars.

CHAPTER 5

Global Growth

5
GLOBAL GROWTH

TO THE REGION

As the eighties drew to a close and a new decade approached, the winds of progress and expansion began to swirl around Hope Haven. The tumultuous seventies refined the ministry. The eighties were years of rebuilding, solidifying, and seeking. The tone of the nineties can be described in one word: expansion. It was a decade of bringing programs and services to other states and even countries.

Two new adult residential programs were the main drivers of all the regional growth. The Community Supervised Assisted Living Arrangement (CSALA) program brought people with disabilities into an apartment training program and taught them independent living skills. The pilot program in Rock Valley was so successful that in 1990, Hope Haven opened a second CSALA apartment program in Rock Rapids, Iowa. At first there was some resistance from other people living in the apartment complex, but the community soon embraced their new neighbors.

A second residential program launched in the early nineties with the addition of two group homes called Westview Homes. These homes served people with severe disabilities whose care required several highly trained staff. Before Hope Haven offered this program, these people had to live outside their community because their care needs were so specialized. When Hope Haven opened Westview Homes, it provided the opportunity for twelve adults with severe disabilities to return to their home community. This program, along with the CSALA program, greatly expanded the scope of residential services offered by Hope Haven.

To support these new programs, the Hope Haven Support Foundation began their first capital campaign, with a goal of raising $600,000 to fund the building of Westview Homes and expand the Work Training Program, later called Parkview Industries. As all this growth was happening in Iowa, the out-of-state requests for these kinds of services began rolling in. The CSALA programs were so successful at helping people with disabilities learn life skills and live semi-independently that parents from around the region began contacting Hope Haven and asking them to bring the program to their towns. One of the places that reached out was Edgerton, Minnesota. The Hope Haven leadership team looked at the opportunity of expanding into Minnesota and discussed the pros and cons of crossing state lines. They sought the Lord's guidance and determined that He was opening the door for Hope Haven to expand into a neighboring state. Even though Edgerton was the community that got the ball rolling, the county wanted Hope Haven to start with a group home in Pipestone, Minnesota.

Anytime you do something pioneering, a few arrows are bound to be shot your way. This is true of Hope Haven's first group home in Pipestone. The leadership team met with city officials numerous times, but after Hope Haven purchased the home and began remodeling, the neighbors started pushing back. They were worried that property values would drop if a group home for people with disabilities came into the neighborhood. There were neighborhood and town hall meetings where Hope Haven staff heard questions like "Shouldn't they be in a more controlled setting?" Yet that's not what Hope Haven's ministry is about. It's a community-based program where people with disabilities live and interact in the community the same way everyone else does. There was every earthly indication to the Hope Haven team that this group home wasn't a good idea. In spite of the staunch resistance, they knew God was opening this door so they walked through it. In the end, the only person who kept resisting was a next door neighbor lady.

A few months after three Hope Haven clients moved into their new home, an overflowing toilet and the need for a plunger changed her tune. Her bathroom toilet became clogged and the other neighbors weren't around, so she had no choice except to ask her Hope Haven neighbors if they had a plunger. One of the residents, Jerry, not only offered her a plunger but also volunteered to go to her house and help unplug her toilet. After that, she became a great neighbor. This story so beautifully illustrates the way that communities and people who previously resisted group homes and apartment training programs softened to their new Hope Haven neighbors once they got to know them as individuals. From that point, Hope Haven established two more group homes in Pipestone before finally moving into Edgerton. This kind of growth, expansion, and overcoming of challenges is the definition of the nineties.

TO THE NATIONS

When we're sensitive to the Lord's guidance, He has a way of surprising us with opportunities. In 1991, God opened yet another door for Hope Haven to step out in faith and ask the question "What can we do to help?" It all began when Hope Haven board member, John Runia, went to the Dominican Republic on a short-term mission trip. As he and his wife were driving to church, they came upon a man and his young daughter. The father had laid her in the tall grass along the road. John picked the girl up and took her to church where she sat on his lap during the service. After church, John had to leave her in the same spot in the grass until her father came back. This broke John's heart. He learned that the young girl couldn't walk due to paralysis, and she spent most of her days in a windowless shack. Other than asking her father or brother to carry her, she couldn't move independently. God used that young lady to speak deeply to John's heart. He returned home to the United States, but the thought of that girl crawling alongside the road wouldn't leave his mind. When John came home to Iowa, he went to see David. John shed tears as he told him this story. Then he pointed his large hand at David and asked, "What are you going to do about it?"

By this time, Hope Haven was the regional leader in disability services, recognized nationally for many of its programs. Why take the time and focus of senior leadership away from this booming business to fly one wheelchair to the Dominican Republic and try to find one girl? It would've been easier not to do it. It would've been easier to say, "We're plenty busy here." Yet Hope Haven is about inclusion and changing the culture so people with disabilities are accepted and valued. That doesn't stop at the border of the United States. As Christians, how could we look the other way at this need?

David and the executive team talked amongst themselves and agreed, "We can do this. Let's buy a wheelchair and take it to her." Hope Haven purchased a $300 wheelchair from a medical supply shop in Orange City. Then Kent Eknes, Hope Haven board president at the time, and Calvin Helmus, who then served as the associate director of operations, were charged with getting it to the Dominican Republic. When it came time for airport security, their resourcefulness led to Cal pushing Kent through security and to the gate in order to get the wheelchair on the plane. As soon as they landed in the Dominican Republic, they began searching for the girl John told them about. Sadly, they never found her. She and her family were likely seasonal workers from Haiti who rarely stayed in one place for long. Kent and Calvin had no trouble finding someone else who needed the wheelchair. They gave it to a young man named Franklin who was totally dependent on other people to carry him around. After getting his wheelchair, Franklin could go wherever he wanted to go without asking for help.

While on this trip to the Dominican Republic, Calvin and Kent also connected with an organization called Rehab Center International. They offered services for people with disabilities, and they also had a work training program where people with special needs grew rooftop gardens, raised hydroponic vegetables, and assembled pens for the

Bic company. It was good work and the employees were paid fairly. The only problem was the electricity got shut off every day because the government wanted to save money. When the electricity was off, it was dark and the machines didn't run. Hope Haven helped solve this problem by purchasing a generator that was big enough to power the facility for days at a time. This dramatically increased their productivity and helped more people with special needs engage in meaningful work. Once Calvin and Kent returned to the United States, they agreed God was calling Hope Haven to action and they better pay attention.

The mission and vision of Hope Haven had been revisited prior to Kent and Calvin going to the Dominican Republic, and they agreed there was nothing in that mission or vision that restricted the way Hope Haven operated geographically. In the end, the decision to officially start Hope Haven International Ministries (HHIM) came from recognizing a need and wanting to be part of the solution. The leaders of Hope Haven asked God to guide them according to His will. Of course, there were obstacles. Finances were tight, people were resistant, and time was stretched. Yet Hope Haven chose to respond because there were voices calling out, voices of people in other countries that they didn't yet know.

In the early 1990s, things were moving quickly at Hope Haven. There were capital campaigns, the building of new programs, starting new group homes, and expanding into other states. So why go to another continent, to another country, and chase international ministry? The answer is simple. If God calls His people to action, they must make room for it to be done. Hope Haven's staff trusted that if God called them to something, He would give them the capacity to think things through. They believed He would supply the resources to carry out this act of faith, and that included money, personnel, and more.

It was also the culture of Hope Haven. We love because He first loved us, and we are always willing to go to the people whose needs aren't being met. When the chance to distribute wheelchairs in other countries arrived, it was a natural fit. People in the Dominican Republic or Romania are people just like us. They have value in God's eyes. Our prayer was, "Lord, it seems like this is an opportunity we can step through, but we can't do this without staying focused on who You are."

In the fall of 1989, the Lord opened yet another door to international ministry. A team from Hope Haven was invited by the Romanian government to tour their nursing homes and orphanages. This team included foundation board president Joe Van Tol, pastor Phil Sneller, then CEO David VanNingen, and others. What they witnessed was revolting. One nursing home, located in the remote countryside, was a two-story, concrete building with no elevator or ramp for the residents who lived on the upper floor. The doors weren't wide enough for a wheelchair to go through, and the whole place reeked of feces and urine. After all they saw on this trip, the team knew Hope Haven had to get involved. If the experiences in the Dominican Republic were the initial spark, the time in Romania stoked that spark into the roaring fire that is Hope Haven International Ministries. A team went back to Romania the following year to bring wheelchairs and build a ramp so the residents could get outside of the nursing home and enjoy some fresh air.

The ministry opportunity in the Dominican Republic was clear, but Romania wasn't as easy to figure out because the country's government leadership was constantly changing. To solve this problem, Hope Haven began connecting with Romanian volunteers who found people who needed wheelchairs. The next step was figuring out how to ship the chairs to their destination. The Hope Haven team learned all of these things the hard way; customs, shipping, logistics. There's not a manual for starting an international wheelchair ministry, but rather many instances of trusting God and figuring out the next best step. Hope Haven exists in an environment that welcomes the opportunity to pioneer. It's rooted in a culture that understands that God gives us gifts, and we have a responsibility to use those talents for the good of others. Hope Haven International Ministries wasn't the result of any one person's vision, it was born out of a community where people honored God and wanted to give because He's given to them.

The goal was to help people with disabilities be included as a valuable member of society, just like everyone else. To change culture by helping society see the value of people with disabilities. The wheelchair became the chosen tool to accomplish these goals because it removes people from isolation. It literally lifts someone out of the dirt and into a seat of dignity and opportunity. Getting a wheelchair meant they could take themselves outside and enjoy the sunshine. They could go to the market and help sell family wares. They could go to school. The chair became the gateway to a new existence full of individual choices, dignity, and recognition of their full, God-given potential.

In 1994, Hope Haven International Ministries was officially launched. From the beginning, it was a volunteer-driven ministry funded solely by gifts, grants, and donations. To grow HHIM's impact, the next step was collecting as many wheelchairs as possible. In the United States, thousands of wheelchairs are discarded every year. They aren't like cars. They don't get traded in at the doctor's office. They're usually either kept or thrown away so HHIM began organizing wheelchair drives to collect used or discarded wheelchairs. After volunteers restored them to like-new condition, they were distributed to individuals with disabilities throughout the world.

In 1996, Hope Haven officially opened operations in Romania with the hiring of David and Marianna Nyquest. The hiring of staff prompted the opening of several new programs and initiatives in Romania. By 1997, so many wheelchairs were being collected that the need for volunteers to refurbish them outgrew the wheelchair repair workshop housed inside of Hope Haven's administrative building. In an innovative effort to find volunteers in more communities, Hope Haven began establishing volunteer wheelchair repair workshops throughout the tri-state area. On a strong year, HHIM distributed 8000-10,000 wheelchairs, so the workshops were busy trying to keep up with demand. The volunteers who work in Hope Haven's wheelchair workshops are amazing people. Many of the men who serve are retired farmers and some of them volunteer over 2000 hours per year. That's a full time job! A number of them have gone on wheelchair distribution trips because they wanted to see where their work goes and meet the people it impacts.

CLIENT STORY: ROMANIAN FAMILY

In 2006, Hope Haven Director of Development Mark Siemonsma took a small team to Romania for a wheelchair distribution trip. As the team worked in the rural countryside, they visited a small, sod house made from mud and straw bricks. These sorts of homes are common in rural areas because they're cheap to construct and easy to add on to. Often, families add extra rooms as they need them, either for more children or to care for aging parents.

This family was caring for their grandfather who'd fallen down and broken his back, becoming paralyzed from the waist down. The man was a former soldier who fought for Romania before the communist takeover of 1947. His small room was hardly big enough for a bed, a tiny table, and a chair. He was totally bedridden and couldn't get up to use the bathroom. As team members poked their heads in to say hello, the overwhelming smell of urine and feces nearly caused them to vomit.

The physical therapist on the team was able to work with this man and bring him outside to enjoy some fresh air as he was fitted for his new wheelchair. Suddenly, the man began to cry. No one could figure out what was going on. Had something happened? Was he hurt? Mark asked the man what was wrong. Through the interpreter, the Romanian grandfather replied, "I've been waiting 40 years for the Americans to come and help. And today you came." His tears were ones of joy.

In just a few years, the global demand for wheelchairs became so large that the ministry reached a point where it couldn't ship the number of needed wheelchairs unless the budget grew too. Even though the Hope Haven Foundation put thousands of dollars behind the wheelchair ministry, more partners were needed to meet the overwhelming need. To solve this problem, HHIM began challenging organizations and corporations to sponsor wheelchairs. At that time, the ministry gave away one wheelchair for every $50 contributed and sent that donor a card showing the person who received their sponsored chair. This program was very successful and funded the distribution of more wheelchairs than ever before. Grant writing, like the Rotary International's Global Grant Program, also became an important part of HHIM's budget.

MILESTONES AND MEANING

The growth of Hope Haven International Ministries happened in conjunction with some major milestones happening domestically. As a direct result of this campaign, a new sheltered workshop was established in Sibley, Iowa. This was the first real work skills site outside of Rock Valley. At this location, about thirty clients did loom weaving as well as assembly and packaging work.

The mid-nineties, especially 1995, was a significant year of growth for Hope Haven. Prior to this time, the children's services numbers were quite low. There were residential programs that served between twenty-five to thirty children, but nowhere near the number served during the years of Hope Haven School. That all changed when the Hope Haven staff noticed a pressing need for behavioral services for at-risk children within the public school system. Hope Haven started after-school programs in Spirit Lake, Estherville, and Spencer. This program was later named EMBARK (Enlightening and Modifying Behaviors with At Risk Kids). Eventually, it expanded to eight school districts and reignited the children's services division of Hope Haven.

As the decade progressed, more and more programs were added to Hope Haven's roster of services. In 1996, the first of four waiver homes opened in Rock Valley. As the number of programs grew, the community's support of Hope Haven's ministry continued to grow as well. In 1997, annual gifts to the Hope Haven Foundation exceeded $1 million. The Lord continued to provide financial resources and personnel to meet the growing budget demands of the ministry.

CLIENT STORY: THE DEN HARTOG BROTHERS

In the beginning, Bruce and Duane Den Hartog seemed just like other boys. Their parents, Paul and Joan Den Hartog of Orange City, proudly talk of the boys' early years spent riding bicycles, making friends in the neighborhood, and learning many skills "right on schedule."

Then, Duane was held back in kindergarten. When he finished, he still wasn't ready for first grade. After some cognitive testing, he was found to have a mental disability. Young Duane needed a special education program, but in the 1950s that meant leaving home to "board" with another family several towns away. Certainly, not an ideal option for the close-knit family.

Meanwhile, Bruce was an adorable 2-year old who won Orange City's 1957 "cute baby" contest. However, he didn't talk a lot and when he reached kindergarten he was sent for similar testing. Coming to grips with the reality of raising two sons with disabilities was challenging for Paul and Joan, yet they knew their sons were capable of leading thriving, purposeful lives.

As teens, Duane and Bruce helped with their family landscaping business, but they yearned to be in the workforce earning a competitive wage. In the 1970s, the brothers were introduced to Hope Haven, and the ministry greatly impacted their daily life. Duane participated in the developing Work Training Program, and Bruce, six years his junior, joined a bit later.

At the Work Training Center (WTC), they mastered increasingly complex skills, began specializing in hitch pin production, and excelled at every aspect of the manufacturing process. In 1998, WTC changed both its focus and name and became Double HH Manufacturing, an integrated, competitive company. Duane and Bruce were proud to be a part of the transition. Today, Double HH Manufacturing is one of the largest producers of hitch pins in the United States and a national model of training for work in the real world. The brothers have helped manufacture nearly 10 million Double HH signature pins. Outside of work, Bruce and Duane enjoy enthusiastically supporting their favorite sports teams and working in the woodshop that their brother Jerry customized for their safety.

"I like working and making friends," Duane said. Bruce explained that his favorite job is "bending handles for the hitch pins."

"They are very proud to be employees at Double HH where they are a part of an integrated workforce, and we are glad to have had dependable and dedicated employees, like Bruce and Duane, producing quality products for the company," the Double HH Plant Manager commented.

Though one of the brothers is now retired, the legacy of the Den Hartog brothers at Double HH Manufacturing continues to inspire all who are witness to their positive attitudes and tremendous work ethic.

Another pioneering event occurred in 1998, when the Work Training Center officially moved into a new building in the Rock Valley industrial park and changed its name to Double HH Manufacturing. Double HH needed a new facility in order to grow, so that's the move the Hope Haven board voted to make. As it grew, Double HH had some trouble with regulators who didn't think a non-profit could manage a profitable business, so Hope Haven had to educate the state regulators who supervised those operations. Many legislators and other state government officials came to visit the facility and were amazed to see the success and growth. They eventually came around to the idea of Hope Haven, a non-profit organization, owning and managing Double HH Manufacturing, a profitable business.

At the time, a non-profit entity owning a profitable business was unheard of in the human services sector. Today, the profits from Double HH Manufacturing are used to underwrite other programs at Hope Haven, accounting for roughly one fourth of the ministry's annual budget. A business that is world-famous for producing hitch pins is quite literally the hitch pin that holds Hope Haven's finances together, allowing the ministry to grow and continue meeting the needs of God's people. A new name and a new location propelled the business to greater heights as production and sales soared. After it moved to the new building in the industrial park, Double HH Manufacturing truly blossomed into a leader in its field.

The Law of the Harvest states that what one sows, so they shall reap. In the nineties, a lot of sowing was done. Hope Haven sowed into residential programs, children's services, Double HH Manufacturing, Hope Haven International Ministries, the Hope Haven Support

Foundation and so much more. Communities within Iowa, the tri-state region, and other parts of the world were changing the way they embraced people with disabilities because of the doors God opened for Hope Haven. The refining of the seventies, the rebuilding of the eighties, and the massive growth of the nineties set Hope Haven on a course of expansion and multiplication as it looked toward the new millennium.

Sustainability and Momentum

6
SUSTAINABILITY AND MOMENTUM

TEN THOUSAND REASONS

Every spring, a farmer plants tiny seeds deep in the fresh, warm soil of his field, sowing each one with faith that it will grow. The farmer plants in faith and harvests with gratitude. In the same way, Hope Haven sowed seeds in the nineties, trusting that God would bring those seeds to maturity. The story of the 2000s is exactly that. Momentum, scaling, multiplication, and maturity.

In the year 2000, Hope Haven served 1211 people with disabilities at forty-two program sites in twenty-two communities. By 2001, total program enrollment grew to 1439 children and adults, the largest in Hope Haven's history up until that point. Just a few years later, in 2003, the $10 million capital campaign that began in 1998 wrapped up its fundraising efforts with total contributions of $13 million. The overwhelming success of the capital campaign reaffirmed that the Hope Haven Society was on the same page as the ministry's leadership as far as mission and vision. It indicated to Hope Haven that people were once again willing to walk side-by-side with them in serving God's people.

Prior to the start of HHIM, financial support for the organization primarily came from a five-state area. With the genesis of the international ministry, support began to come in from around the country. The wheelchair ministry put new life, energy, and vitality into the Hope Haven Foundation's fundraising efforts. In 2001, this financial support helped the ministry hit the milestone of 10,000 total wheelchairs distributed, and many of them were Hope Haven's proprietary "KidChair" design.

Since the beginning of HHIM, there was always a lack of children's wheelchairs collected but a lot of need for them at distributions. Never afraid to pioneer something new, Hope Haven talked with a group of engineering students from Dordt University who agreed to take on the project of designing a children's wheelchair.

There were a few important requirements. First, it had to be easy to manufacture in many different countries around the world. Second, it had to be very tough. Finally, it had to accommodate a range of growth so the child who received it wouldn't instantly need a different one as they got older. The first children's wheelchair design was made of plastic and bent metal tubing. There wasn't a weld on it, and it could accommodate up to 115 pounds of growth. It could also take heavy use and get around in difficult conditions. In short, it checked all the right boxes. That was in 1999, and by 2001, the design had been in production for over a year.

Even in times of wide-reaching growth and expansion, quality care for each person is the number one priority. Hope Haven employee Mark Richard played an important role in setting up the way the distributions were run. From the beginning, every person was custom fit to their chair. Mark knew it wasn't good enough to plop somebody in a chair and send them off. It may work for a little bit, but in the long run, it could spell disaster for the recipient. At a Hope Haven wheelchair distribution, every person is custom fit to their chair by a physical therapist. They also receive a follow-up call or visit about their wheelchair and are connected with a local church. It takes about an hour per person to assemble each chair and fit it to its new owner.

The stories of the people met at these distributions are mind-boggling. One young girl named Luce had been abandoned by her parents at a year old because she was disabled. She'd spent most of her life in village care, but when she came to the Hope Haven distribution to get her first wheelchair, she was determined to get into that chair all by herself. She struggled, pushed, and maneuvered herself into the seat, and it was a near perfect fit. With a big smile on her face, the first thing she said was, "Now I can go to school with my friends."

Every chair that has been given away has a story like this. For one person, a chair may mean the chance to go to school. For someone else, it could mean gaining dignity and respect among their community. With a wheelchair, they can become part of the family business and sell goods at the marketplace. A wheelchair opens the door for them to work and earn an income. The success of the wheelchair distribution program in the early 2000s is representative of what was happening across the whole Hope Haven organization. It was multiplying quickly but the focus was still on caring for people well and cultivating their individuality.

THE MORE

Growth, innovation, and advancement were abundant in every branch of Hope Haven's ministry. Under Chief Manufacturing Officer Loy Van't Hul's leadership, Double HH Manufacturing expanded its product line in 2001 when it began producing the Lockease hitch pin. This clever pin solved a simple problem farmers had fought for years. In their rough and bumpy fields, the farmers grain carts or other farm trailers would often come unhooked from the tractor. In the design of a basic hitch pin, the pin drops through the loop and a small, metal clip is pushed through a small hole drilled in the bottom of the pin. Well, sometimes those clips work their way out amidst the bumps of the field. With the Lockease hitch pin, a large, square clip was included in the design of the pin so that the operator simply dropped the pin through the hole and swung the square part of the clip around to lock it into place. Then the hitch pin was securely fastened and couldn't shake out of place. It solved a serious problem for farmers because grain carts and other equipment that come unhooked not only waste time, but are also quite dangerous. Just as Hope Haven meets the practical needs of people with disabilities, Double HH Manufacturing's products solve real, tangible needs for those in agriculture.

The growth pattern continued in 2006 when the Hope Haven Foundation began a new $20 million dollar capital campaign. The funds generated by this campaign were for a few specific projects: (1) the remodeling of the main Hope Haven administrative building in Rock Valley so HHIM could use the space previously occupied by the Work Training Center, (2) provide operating support for client homes and scholarships, and (3) to invest in the future of Hope Haven by increasing the overall endowment of the foundation.

In 2007, HHIM reached the milestone of one million documented hours of volunteer support for the ministry. Since the beginning, it was completely volunteer driven and funded through benevolent dollars, and those one million hours of volunteer time proved how strongly the volunteer community embraced the cause. In addition to Rock Valley's support of the wheelchair program, a second source of support came from an unexpected place - the South Dakota State Penitentiary. At any one time, approximately forty inmates are working on refurbishing used wheelchairs to like-new condition from within the concrete walls of the Sioux Falls-based prison.

These men spend seven hours per day restoring wheelchairs to like-new condition and enjoy using their time to contribute to the world in a positive way. Many of them also love the opportunity to be away from their cell. The prison schedule dictates that when they're not eating or using their daily one hour allotment of time outside, they must be in their cell. That is unless they're involved in a work program. To be accepted to the HHIM work program, they must apply and go through an interview process. Even though other jobs within the prison pay higher wages, they choose to work in the wheelchair shop because they believe in the mission of the ministry. These forty faithful men are the backbone of HHIM's wheelchair refurbishment program.

VOLUNTEER STORY: BEAR PACE

Though he's confined to the bounds of the South Dakota State Peniten-
tiary, Bear (Durke) Pace has invested his recent years in blessing children
around the world who are locked in their homes by poverty and disability.
He wanted to learn to sew in high school "but my football buddies made
too much fun," explained this talented craftsman of fabric for wheelchair
cushions, seats, armrests, and totes.

"It feels great to do something to help these young ones! Anything that gets
inmates helping others makes them feel so much better about themselves.
Most of these guys, deep down, are really good guys," Bear said.

The wheelchair refurbishing workshops, the hours spent doing
wheelchair drives, and the efforts made to distribute them all over
the world show how people wanted to get involved in meeting the
needs of people with disabilities. In fact, the wheelchair refurbishing
workshops popped up because groups of people in various communities wanted to contribute in a meaningful way.

The momentum continued to build into 2009 as Hope Haven
reached an annual budget of $23 million which was used to serve
the 1276 people involved in its programs. In addition to the budget
for domestic operations, the ministry efforts meant that over 7500
children's wheelchairs were manufactured, 750 of which were made
in the Guatemala workshop that had been established in 2008. After
fifteen years of ministry, HHIM had distributed over 84,000 wheelchairs to children and adults around the world.

With the dawning of 2010, the momentum from the first decade of
the new millennium flowed into the second one. From 2010 to 2017,
Hope Haven's annual budget went from approximately $20 million

— 104 —

to more than $40 million. This growth in budget and scope of services happened as Hope Haven began taking over management of several smaller organizations in the area.

On January 1, 2010, Hope Haven officially began managing The Achievement Center in Worthington, Minnesota. This workshop served about 130 clients and employed 24 staff members. In 2014, Hope Haven took over management of Echo Plus which had locations in Estherville and Spirit Lake, Iowa. In July of 2015, Hope Haven became partners with Sunshine Services in Spencer, Iowa. The 2018 merger with Faith, Hope, and Charity of Storm Lake, Iowa expanded Hope Haven's staff and services even further, serving over 80 new clients in children's services from ages six to twenty-one and bringing 120 new staff members onto the team.

Under David VanNingen's leadership, Hope Haven took on the day-to-day management of these locations so they wouldn't close and the people they served wouldn't have to leave their communities. God opened the door for the ministry to share their resources, knowledge, and leadership with these other programs that were struggling. In fact, the Hope Haven executive team mentored the leaders of Sunshine Services for nearly fifteen years before taking over management of the program. Expanding in this way and meeting practical needs continued to be a guiding principle for Hope Haven's leadership team as they sought the Lord's guidance on how to best help the people who were served by these organizations. Ultimately, becoming partners and taking over management of the facilities was the best option.

MILESTONES AND MEANING

As Hope Haven continued to mature into the vast ministry it is today, the scale of growth was always balanced with a belief in doing things well. Each new addition of a service or a program was done thoughtfully and with great discernment. Yet the leadership was never afraid to act once they were certain of God's leading. For example, HHIM opened the first international wheelchair repair and manufacturing facility in Guatemala in 2008. The long-term strategic planning of the ministry involved opening workshops in other countries, and Guatemala was the first international location where the chairs were actually assembled. With this expansion came the desire to grow thoughtfully and with respect to the culture. Hope Haven engaged the people of Guatemala to respond to the needs of people with disabilities within their own country. It was a community-based approach, just like it was in Rock Valley and numerous other communities in the tri-state region.

The success of Hope Haven's community-based programs was truly on display in the spring of 2014. The river was rising, a dam broke in Minnesota, the rains came without ceasing, and the town of Rock Valley was faced with an imminent flood. People were out in the rain filling sandbags when the city councilmen got everyone's attention and said a certain part of the town needed to be evacuated. Hope Haven's Redwood Court Homes were in that part of town, and by the time Hope Haven CEO David VanNingen got there, buses were already parked in front of the facility and townspeople were walking Hope Haven clients away from the rising waters and towards the buses. The whole community was responding to the needs of their neighbors, and it didn't matter that those neighbors were clients of Hope Haven, they were still their neighbors. David thought to himself "Hope Haven really works. This is no longer about people having disabilities, it's about people helping their neighbors. I can still see two people, one on each side of a Hope Haven client, assuring them it would be ok, helping them on the bus and sitting with them." He stood in front of the group home that night and watched true community happen.

The clients were evacuated to Faith Reformed Church and once again, their neighbors were there. They rode with them on the bus to make sure they wouldn't become too upset by the changes and unpredictability. They provided them with comfort. It was powerful. It was everything that we had worked for as a community at Hope Haven.

There's been a lot of struggle as Hope Haven reached outside of Rock Valley. The Pipestone story repeated itself over and over again. People are all desperately scared of the unknown and people with disabilities, in some cases, were the unknown. So much so that Hope Haven came up with a process to introduce people with disabilities to the community. What happened the night of the flood is Hope Haven's true vision. Cultivating places where people are committed to helping the creation of God through their gifts, talents and contributions. We must live boldly, embracing the belief that what Hope Haven has isn't ours to keep, it's ours to give.

VOLUNTEER STORY: BRETT ROBY

Brett Roby's contagious smile is famous around the halls of Hope Haven. Yet life did not start off smoothly for Brett. When he came to Hope Haven in 1986, he'd been in over twenty different foster and group homes and hadn't achieved expectations at any of them. Placement in these homes did not fit his needs, and Hope Haven was his last resort for a community-based program. The next step would've been a locked, ward-style facility. Brett thrived within the warm, welcoming environment, and his former behavioral issues disappeared. In fact, he became a model employee and community member. Today, he serves on Hope Haven's janitorial staff and is a full-fledged employee.

"When I came to Hope Haven, I finally found a future," Brett said.

Through the years, Brett's Grandma kept contact with him. She encouraged him to get to know Jesus and join a church. Brett joined Faith Reformed Church and began meeting with his pastor regularly. Through these meetings, he came to know Jesus as his Lord and Savior. On April 2, 1989, Brett made his profession of faith. Today, he loves to share how God is working in his life.

"I found out that good works do not get you into heaven. Instead, it's the grace of the Lord Jesus Christ," Brett said.

Brett is an active member of Faith Reformed Church. He loves to sing hymns and visit with his fellow churchgoers. You can ask him about any date, statistic, or major event in sports, and he'll instantly give a thorough, accurate answer. He knows all about James Bond, the politics of Argentina, and the date of the Cubs' last World Series win.

Brett is beloved in the community. During the school year, you can find him faithfully attending every sporting event at Western Christian High School. He leads cheers during basketball games and is friends with all the players. When he's not at work or a sporting event, he enjoys riding his bike around Rock Valley or visiting the local library.

"I'm just glad to be part of Hope Haven and that God is willing to do good work through me. Without Hope Haven, I would've been lost," Brett said.

The group homes that were damaged during the flood were rebuilt by August. In 2015, Hope Haven reached a pinnacle of its highest enrollment ever at 2064 children and adults. While client service was at its highest, another government change happened when payment for client services switched from Medicare to Managed Care. The new funding streams meant Hope Haven had to change everything about the way it billed for client services. It also increased the amount of time it took for the ministry to get paid for services it provided. Even though he was reaching the end of his time at Hope Haven, David VanNingen stayed on as CEO until the organization found its way to more stable ground within the Managed Care landscape. The consistency of his leadership and of many other senior leaders helped Hope Haven navigate these turbulent waters of finances and government regulation.

It was around this time that many of the senior leaders on Hope Haven's executive team were nearing retirement. To make the transition as smooth as possible, these leaders gave the board a two to three year notice of retirement. This was a core group of leaders that were all about the same age, and they didn't want to remove their years of experience from the agency all at once. The leadership team navigated this transition strategically by putting together a matrix laying out who was leaving and when. Next, each leader began to mentor the person who would fill their role. One of the key leaders that retired was long-time CEO David VanNingen. In 2017, David retired after thirty-one years of humble service and leadership at Hope Haven.

This was a landmark change for the ministry. When David became CEO in 1986, Hope Haven operated on a $3.7 million budget and served approximately 240 clients. By the time he retired, the annual budget had grown to over $40 million and served over 1400 clients. Under three decades of David's leadership, Hope Haven to grow, changed, adapted, and pioneered. Countless new programs of service were established and a few of them were discontinued. The fluidity of David's steady leadership and compelling vision joined with God's provision and a caring staff grew Hope Haven beyond what the founding fathers ever dreamed it could become. From its humble beginnings as a school serving eleven students, the Hope Haven of today is a pioneering force in all aspects of service to people with disabilities.

The person who took over the reins after David's retirement had large shoes to fill. They needed to be a leader with vision, enthusiasm, passion, and above all, faith in God. To guide the ministry into its future required the right person who understood the difficulties of running a service-based ministry that also owns a profitable manufacturing business and ships wheelchairs all over the world. The size and scope of Hope Haven's operations are enough to boggle the minds of most, but in His perfect faithfulness, the Lord provided Matt Buley as Hope Haven's sixth CEO and executive director.

Invitation

THE INVITATION

We've reached the end of the historical portion of this narrative. Thank you for taking the time to learn about our story origins, who we are, where we've been, and who we serve. Now, we'd love to share with you our hopes for the future. We invite you to join the story and come along for the ride. The Lord has done incredible things through Hope Haven, and we would be honored for you to walk this path alongside us. Today, the services offered by this organization are completely different from the services offered in 1964, yet the heart and values remain the same.

Yes, a few things have changed since that first coffee conversation in 1959. These days, the meeting place looks a bit different. The projects are bigger and so is the budget. Yet the conversations still begin by asking the original question "What can we do to help?" We were still drinking lots of coffee, serving our community, working hard, and stepping through the doors God puts on our path.

As we look ahead to the next fifty years of ministry, we challenge you to ask yourself the question "What can I do to help?" As you ponder this question, we invite you into the final chapter of this book where we'll share with you a vision for the way forward. The next fifty years are sure to be just as exciting as the first fifty, and we know the Lord's work through Hope Haven is nowhere close to finished.

The Next Fifty Years

7

THE NEXT FIFTY YEARS

THE WALK AND THE WORK

On August 1, 2017, Matt Buley took over as the sixth CEO and executive director of Hope Haven, and with that transition, a new chapter of Hope Haven's history began. While our hearts and minds remain open to what the Lord brings about next, we want to share a few key initiatives that we predict to be important milestones along Hope Haven's roadmap for the next fifty years. The number of people this ministry serves and the ways it serves them will adapt with the times, but what won't change is our core mission, vision, and values. The faithful people who founded Hope Haven in 1964 and the leadership team of today use the same words to describe the work before us. It's a community of people who love God and walk alongside those with disabilities to help them reach their full potential.

FAITH

Hope Haven's Christian faith will continue on as the guiding light. As Christ followers, we view God as the ultimate good, meaning that everything good comes from Him. Our best ideas, services, outreaches, and pioneering pursuits are from Him. We believe the best of us comes from following Him because He is the best of us. He is the source of all things good, and we love because He first loved us.

ADVOCACY

We're committed to changing how people with disabilities are perceived in the world. Because of this commitment, we'll remain part of the Iowa state legislative discussion as it pertains to funding for people with special needs. The sources of funding for the work done by Hope Haven can be difficult to navigate, and from a federal or a state level, it doesn't always appear that people with disabilities are valued as highly as they should be. Hope Haven envisions being a leader in legislative advocacy to fight those limitations and be a voice for people with disabilities, especially in the realm of funding. This ministry will also continue to partner with organizations that serve people with disabilities with a similar heart and purpose, coming alongside to help them weather the storms of funding shortages, legislative change, and market turbulence.

LEADERSHIP

Hope Haven is continuing to develop a culture of leadership within its staff. Leadership coaching and training is a crucial part of the ministry's work, and Hope Haven will always be about teaching people how to unleash potential in others. In fact, it's our goal that people would come to Hope Haven to learn how to be a leader in the field of disability services. Through Hope Haven's efforts, we envision Rock Valley becoming known as a place where world class leaders come to grow. The founding fathers of this ministry were told that "nothing will grow in the cornfields of Iowa," but history has proven otherwise. We believe this is a place where leaders can come to blossom.

INNOVATION

Since the beginning, Hope Haven has been an innovator in our field and that is not going to change. This inclination to pioneer programs and different kinds of ministry efforts is part of what makes Hope Haven so special. It's also what draws people of wonderful talent to the organization. By God's grace, we'll continue to step through the new doors He places on our path.

MOBILITY

It's been estimated that over 100 million people in the world need a wheelchair and can't get one. Meeting this worldwide need is a significant part of our next fifty years. Our goal is to have wheelchair manufacturing and distribution facilities in additional countries that have an expansive impact on even more countries around them and have wheelchair distribution sites on all seven continents. Excellent work has been happening for years, and we hope to scale it to an even greater level.

VOLUNTEERISM

A crucial part of scaling Hope Haven International Ministries is expanding our team of volunteers. The wheelchair distributions of HHIM are funded solely through benevolent dollars and made possible by the work of wonderful volunteers. Our vision for the future is to engage an even greater group of volunteers to further the work of the wheelchair ministry. We plan to clearly share the volunteer opportunities that exist; like leading wheelchair drives, volunteering at a wheelchair refurbishment workshop, volunteering to help build new KidChairs, or working with Hope Haven to raise money for distributions around the world.

STEWARDSHIP

We seek to be known as leaders and stewards of something much bigger than ourselves. Because we're Christ-followers, the way in which we serve is unique. We believe the precious resources given to us by God are not ours to keep but ours to give. We seek to model a culture that promotes teaching and outpouring of love, knowledge, and skills. Part of this stewardship is caring for the growth of the Hope Haven Support Foundation endowment. This resource directly impacts the amount of work that Hope Haven International Ministries can do throughout the world. Growing the endowment means not only more impact internationally but also greater stability for the work of Hope Haven in the United States.

CORE VALUES

The core values of an organization are the fundamental beliefs deemed essential to its existence. Just as a building missing a crucial support structure cannot stand, an organization without these guiding principles cannot thrive. Hope Haven needs these strong, unwavering commitments in order to remain active and relevant. These are the five core values that will direct Hope Haven's path over the next fifty years.

WE ARE...

CHRIST-FOLLOWERS

Being Christ-followers is imparted into the deepest ethos of Hope Haven. We serve a boundless God, and with Him, all things are possible. There's no end to His love and we are humbled to participate in such abundance. We believe that if we steward His resources well, the growth will follow. Faith in God and His love for every part of His creation is our anchor amongst the turbulence of this world. Because of His great love for us, we believe in giving away as much as possible, holding our resources as stewards rather than owners.

Being Christ-followers also means we are called to love our colleagues as ourselves. In serving the ultimate strength and love, which is God, we are beckoned to be better. To be strong, loving, and accountable to one another. Held to a standard of excellence through truth and grace, we challenge one another to be world-class at our work because we serve God and our work is an offering to Him.

WELCOMING

The word welcoming communicates the power of being positive, authentic, high in emotional intelligence, and self-aware. Every day, we work to ensure Hope Haven is a welcoming place. Whether you walk into our lobby as a guest, receive regular services as a client, or encounter us on an international wheelchair distribution, we promise to be the kind of people that extend ourselves for others.

For a Hope Haven staff member, this welcoming culture means you have access to your leadership. It also means knowing that you matter to your fellow colleagues. This is a workplace where you can belong. For our clients, this culture of warm welcome and open hearts means this is a place where you can be comfortable. It's an environment where you'll be guided and empowered to reach your fullest potential. As we look ahead to the future, we pray this spirit of welcome creates an environment where Hope Haven clients, staff, and supporters continue to gather and serve one another in a spirit of love for God and for one another.

ACCOUNTABLE

At Hope Haven, accountability is a trademark of the way we work together and conduct business. Our staff members hold one another to a high standard, and we often have conversations centered around the question "What does it mean to be community?"

For our clients, a culture of accountability means they're going to receive the best possible care because the team working alongside them is held to a standard of excellence. It also means that as a staff, we're also going to help our clients be accountable to their God-given responsibility to achieve their highest potential and use their gifts in service to the community. Hope Haven staff recognize the clients' potential and walk alongside each person to help them accomplish their goals. Finally, this pillar of accountability means Hope Haven answers to its results. Whether that means improving existing services or identifying opportunities for new programs, the results show us where we can continue to strive for excellence.

COMPASSIONATE

Merriam-Webster defines compassion as "sympathetic consciousness of others' distress together with a desire to alleviate it." Hope Haven's founding story can be described with this single word. An awareness of distress coupled with a desire to help alleviate the challenge sparked an idea which grew in the Hope Haven School. Today, the ministry is a regional, national, global leader in services for people with disabilities because each step of growth is led by compassion. For our clients, living, learning, and working within a culture of compassion means daily experiences of acceptance, kindness and warmth.

It also means being compassionate towards one another as staff members and supporters. Our staff members tend to be kind and caring. We are there for one another, even when we're not at work. Finally, compassion as a pillar of growth creates a culture where like-minded, compassionate people want to come and work.

INNOVATIVE

This pillar of growth could also include the word "pioneering." To pioneer and innovate simply means to do something in a new way. To go into uncharted territory and figure out the path. Hope Haven's history is full of pioneering events, and we know this pattern will continue long into our future. To do something new takes faith, and as Christ-followers, our faith is in the Lord. We believe He leads us into areas of pioneering, and we follow His guidance as He opens new doors for us to step through.

Part of pioneering is being able to learn and adapt quickly. We seek to be a learning organization where boldness, humility, and ideation coincide to produce creative new ways of serving our community. We were created by a creating God, and He stirs within each of us the desire to chart new paths. Part of innovating is failing, but because we're a culture of compassion and accountability, our staff knows that "failing" isn't an end point but rather a stepping stone to a solution.

OUR CHALLENGE

Dear Reader,

Thank you for taking the time to walk with us through our story. It's one that is continuing to unfold by God's grace. Whether you're a current employee of Hope Haven, a client, the family member of a client, a financial contributor, or someone who has never engaged with us before, please remember this: we are a group of people who love God and operate under the guidance of the Holy Spirit to serve people with disabilities. There's no way to know what changes we'll see next in the world, in culture, or in our industry. We continue to plan, but more than that, we continue submitting to the One who directs us. We are better because we plan, but we're best because God is leading us. Living without Christ is like living without gravity, and we wouldn't know what we were doing if we weren't anchored by Him.

The first fifty years of our history were incredible, and we are filled with hopeful expectation for the next fifty. Looking back at all the Lord has done through a ministry that began as a ten student school in a small Iowa town, we can't wait to see how He transforms the Hope Haven of today. We continue to ask one another important questions. How can we better live out Godly community? How do we connect with people and where does that spur us to go next? A story of God's faithfulness and a community's obedience has been told within these pages, and that story isn't over yet.

Conclusion

CONCLUSION

We've come to the end of our time together, but that doesn't mean the story is over. In fact, it is just the beginning! Have you been touched by the work Hope Haven is doing? If the Lord has placed a calling on your heart to help people with disabilities, please know there's a place for you here. A place to serve, volunteer, give, or work. If it's giving, know that stewardship is the heartbeat of Hope Haven. We hold each gift with diligence, and it will be maximized for the work of God's kingdom in the service of His precious people who have special needs.

If your ministry is through prayer, please pray for the hearts and minds of our clients, staff and supporters. Also pray that our leadership team continues to be sensitive to the Lord's direction. If you serve best through volunteering, we encourage you to find a way to serve within your community. There are many opportunities for volunteers to get involved in Hope Haven projects happening around the region and the world. Above all, we encourage you to cultivate your own personal relationship with Jesus. He is the source of all that is good, and we know that as long as we continue to follow Him, the future is very, very bright.

We'll leave you with the question our founders asked so many years ago "What can we do to help?" It's a dangerous question. "What can we do?" It opens the door to all kinds of ways for God to enter in and go to work, both in our hearts and in the world. Hope Haven's story started with this simple yet powerful question. Now, we challenge you to ask yourself the same question and prepare to be amazed as God opens surprising doors in your path. Our history shows us that great things happen when God's people gather over a cup of coffee. If you want to connect with us and play a role in the Hope Haven story of the next fifty years, we'd love to meet you for coffee and a conversation.

Acknowledgements

ACKNOWLEDGEMENTS

We would like to take this opportunity to sincerely thank all of the people who agreed to be interviewed for this project. Hope Haven's history is a colorful tapestry woven from the threads of many voices. We want to thank David VanNingen, John and Mary Van Zanten, Harvey De Jager, Calvin Helmus, Paul Moos, and Matt Buley for offering up their time, knowledge, and talents in service to this project. Mark Siemonsma has our gratitude for initiating and guiding this project to its completion. We also extend a special "thank you" to Marlowe Van Ginkel for being the voice of Hope Haven for so many years and contributing it to this book.

About the Company

ABOUT THE COMPANY

Years before Hope Haven became a reality, it started as the dream of four Midwestern forefathers - and it all began over a cup of coffee.

This group envisioned a future full of possibilities for children in their community with disabilities, and were determined to bring their ideas to life. After years of dedication and a series of uphill battles, Hope Haven opened its doors to eleven children in 1964.

From our beginnings in Northwest Iowa, we've grown and adapted - expanding in both services and scope. Today, we're present in counties around the Midwest, and our International Ministries impacts the lives of people in over 100 countries.

We continue to develop and refine programs to accommodate ongoing needs, and remain committed to empowering others to recognize, appreciate and share their talents.

To join our mission, please contact us at www.HopeHaven.org